Doreen Smith

Violin Sight-Reading

Book 2

Music Department
OXFORD UNIVERSITY PRESS
Oxford and New York

NOTE

These graded sight-reading pieces for the violin are designed to provide practice material at all stages. Book 1 begins with the first position and covers the usual examination expectations for the earlier grades. More advanced players will find exercises requiring use of the higher registers, and the need for more technical expertise in book 2.

Fingering and bowing

There are as many fingerings and bowings as there are players. Those marked here are simply one way of performing a piece; they are by no means obligatory. The aim is to give as musical an impression as possible after a brief study of the piece, and to enjoy exploring the instrument.

To the violinist — what to do before you play

Look at:

- The **foreign words** which will suggest the speed, mood, and style.
- The **key signature**: work out your finger patterns on each string.
- The **time signature**: are you going to count in beats, or would it be more helpful to sub-divide each beat?
- **Changes** of key signature or time signature (in higher grades).
- **Unusual** time patterns, accidentals, rests, staccato notes, slurs, and dynamics.
- The **speed**: decide on the speed and count at least one bar before you begin. Count aloud throughout.

Keep going, and try to give an overall impression of the music.

Doreen Smith, 1992

VIOLIN SIGHT-READING, BOOK 2

by DOREEN SMITH

GRADE 6

*2nd position optional

4

Andante con tenerezza

*2nd position optional

Vivo

5

Tempo di minuetto

6

GRADE 7

10

12

15

Lento cantabile

GRADE 8

Slow 'blues' tempo

Allegro scherzando

14

Lento moderato

15

Allegretto giusto

16